UNLOCKING INFINITY

Your Path to Endless Possibilities

BY

Brendan J. Griffin

Acknowledgments

This book, "Unlocking Infinity: Your Path to Endless Possibilities," is the result of a labor of love and an inspirational journey that has left no end. It's a trip that would not have been possible without the assistance, inspiration, and support of numerous exceptional people and resources. As I get to the end of this book, I am incredibly appreciative of their significant contributions to its creation.

In my family

I want to express my sincere gratitude to my family, who have been my staunch pillars of strength and unshakable sources of support. This project has been motivated by your confidence in my creative endeavors and your constant support. I appreciate your support as we travel towards achieving eternity.

My Companions

I am incredibly appreciative of my friends who have provided their ears, their shoulders, and their unshakable companionship during the highs and lows of this artistic journey. I appreciate you being here because it serves as a constant reminder that we are never alone in our pursuits.

My role models

I want to sincerely thank the mentors and advisers who have imparted their experience, insight, and knowledge. The concepts and ideas provided in this book have been significantly influenced by your impact.

The Audience:

I want to express my gratitude to you, the readers. Your curiosity, need for information, and desire for personal development are what make creating a book like this such a worthwhile endeavor. We appreciate you joining us on this adventure, and we hope that the words you find here will help you on your way to realizing your limitless potential.

The Group:

I would like to sincerely thank the hardworking group who helped to produce this book. Your combined efforts, from editors and designers to publishers and marketers, have been essential in realizing our vision.

The Eternal Source

Thank you to the infinite universe, which is the greatest source of creativity and inspiration. We are merely conduits, directing the countless possibilities that are all around us. May we keep searching for answers to the universe's riddles.

Internal Self:

I extend my sincere gratitude to the inner self that strives to develop and expand at all times. The journey to unlocking infinity starts inside each of us, and it develops with each self-reflective thought and deliberate deed.

The combined efforts, hopes, and dreams of many people and influences have culminated in this book. It serves as evidence for the proposition that by working together, we may discover our limitless potential and motivate others to do the same.

With sincere appreciation,

Brendan J. Griffin

ABOUT THE BOOK

Are you prepared to start a trip that will change your life and open up a world of boundless options and potential? "Unlocking Infinity" will lead you to a place where there are no boundaries to growth, where possibilities are as endless as the cosmos itself, and where the horizon is never constrained.

You'll learn the power of the unlimited mindset in this stimulating and motivating book. You'll change from having a fixed viewpoint to having a growth-focused mentality, creating the conditions for both your personal and professional success. Explore the nuances of overcoming limitations that you have placed on yourself and use positivity as a beacon to attract riches into your life.

But this journey doesn't end with a change in thinking. "Unlocking Infinity" launches you into the world of invention and creativity, where you'll discover how to get beyond creative roadblocks, access limitless inspiration, and embrace the revolutionary power of cutting-edge technologies.

The book explores the spiritual world as well as the physical one, directing you toward inner peace and fulfillment. Find the meaning that makes your life more fulfilling, and use mindfulness and meditation techniques to strengthen your connection to your inner self.

"Unlocking Infinity" gives you the adaptability to successfully manage change as it comes with life. This manual shares the techniques for identifying fresh passions and interests, ensuring that your journey is never static but continually changing.

The ending is not the end, but rather the start of something new, inspiring you to tap into your limitless potential and bravely pursue the opportunities that lie ahead. Your path to countless opportunities starts right now.

"Unlocking Infinity" holds the key to opening the doors to your limitless potential. This book is about more than just reading; it's also about living life differently, accepting change, developing creativity, and getting in touch with your inner self. It has to do with releasing your boundless potential.

Are you prepared to go off on your path to limitless possibilities? Opening this book is the first step; the next is to open your mind to the limitless.

Realize your full potential. Activate your life. Activate infinity.

TABLE OF CONTENTS

CHAPTER 6: TECHNOLOGY AND INNOVATION IN THE INFINITE AGE

EXPLORING THE INTERSECTION OF INNOVATION AND PERSONAL GROWTH
THE ROLE OF INNOVATION IN PERSONAL DEVELOPMENT
EMBRACING EMERGING TECHNOLOGIES
THE ROLE OF INNOVATION IN YOUR PERSONAL JOURNEY

CHAPTER 7: SPIRITUAL AWAKENING AND INTERNAL CONTENTMENT

THE SPIRITUAL QUEST FOR MEANING
PRACTISES OF MINDFULNESS AND MEDITATION
OBTAINING BALANCE AND HARMONY IN LIFE

CHAPTER 8: TRANSITIONING TO A NEW CHAPTER

Introduction

Welcome to a voyage that will alter your viewpoint, raise your goals, and give you the ability to realize the boundless potential that exists inside of you. We set out to investigate the profound idea of "Unlocking Infinity" and how it may serve as the compass for the most astonishing chapters of your life in the pages that follow.

Imagine living in a universe where your mental limitations are nothing more than conjecture and where the opportunities that are available to you are as limitless as the cosmos itself. In this dimension, the limitations of self-doubt, fear, and limiting beliefs are replaced with infinite creativity, unflinching drive, and tireless pursuit of your dreams.

This book's thesis is straightforward but profound: You can open up the limitless. The barriers that could have kept you back in the past could be broken by you. The only boundaries you set for yourself exist. Your secret to overcoming those artificial constraints and entering a universe where options are truly limitless is "Unlocking Infinity".

We will go deeply into the skill of adopting the infinite mindset—a mindset that lives on development, creativity, and unrelenting curiosity in the pages that follow. We'll look at ways to overcome self-doubt and discover how to use setbacks as stepping stones on the way to success. You will learn how to tap into the unbounded creativity that is within of you and use it in all facets of your life, from your profession to your hobbies.

In addition, "Unlocking Infinity" is more than simply a book about personal growth; it's also a manual for advancing your job, starting a successful business, and surviving the constantly changing world of innovation and technology. We will look at how these spheres intersect with your journey of personal development.

However, this book is about more than just achieving professional and personal success; it's also about discovering harmony, meaning, and spiritual fulfillment in a society where the need for limitless opportunities can occasionally become overwhelming. We'll delve into the spiritual, mindful, and inner calm realms while directing you toward serenity and enlightenment.

"Unlocking Infinity" is your compass to navigate the immense sea of possibility that awaits you, whether you are an ambitious entrepreneur, a career-driven professional, an artist looking for inspiration, or just someone on a journey for personal growth and purpose.

Your trip starts right here, and as we set out on it together, keep in mind that the infinite is not some far-off horizon; rather, it is the very core of who you are. It's time to open it up and set out on a route leading to countless opportunities. This is "Unlocking Infinity: Your Path to Endless Possibilities."

Chapter 1: Embracing the Infinite Mindset

There is a transformative mindset—a mindset with the capacity to overcome obstacles and lead us to amazing achievements—in a world where restrictions frequently seem to dictate our possibilities. This is the Infinite Mindset, a perspective that radically changes how we see ourselves and the world around us. It doesn't merely urge us to think large and establish ambitious goals.

Understanding the Infinite Mindset

The Infinite Mindset is fundamentally a mode of thinking that transcends boundaries and restrictions. It involves adopting a viewpoint that sees opportunity where others see barriers, and it's an attitude that supports development, invention, and unrelenting curiosity.

Imagine this: You embrace problems with enthusiasm and see them as chances for progress rather than being constrained by the fear of failure or the notion that your abilities are fixed. The Infinite Mindset is characterized by an unshakeable faith in the limitless possibilities that lay ahead.

Shifting from Fixed to Growth Thinking

Understanding the idea of changing from a fixed mindset to a growth mindset is crucial for completely embracing the Infinite Mindset. These phrases were coined by psychologist Carol Dweck to distinguish between two different theories of learning and growth.

• **Fixed Mindset:** People who have a fixed mindset frequently consider intelligence, talents, and skills to be fixed attributes. They frequently avoid difficulties out of concern that they might reveal their weaknesses. Failure is not viewed as an opportunity for learning, but rather as a reflection of their weakness.

• **Growth Mindset:** In contrast, people who have this mindset view obstacles as opportunities to advance. They think they can improve and broaden their skills with hard work, repetition, and patience. They see failure as an opportunity to grow and learn.

The first step on the path to adopting the Infinite Mindset is to be completely honest about where you are right now on this spectrum. Do you often feel constrained by your restrictions and preconceived notions? Or are you enthusiastic to embrace improvement and advancement, welcoming difficulties as stepping stones to your growth?

Cultivating a Positive and Open Mind

It's vital to cultivate positive and open thinking to unleash the limitless within ourselves. On our journey to reaching our full potential, negativity, self-doubt, and a closed-off worldview can be powerful barriers.

Power of Positive Thinking: We'll look at useful methods for encouraging a constructive outlook. You'll discover how to quiet the inner critic that restricts you and swap it out with a positive inner voice that motivates you to take chances and push your comfort zone. You'll be more prepared to meet obstacles with resiliency and ingenuity if you keep an optimistic mindset.

Embracing Curiosity: An open mind is a curious mind, constantly looking to broaden its horizons and unearth fresh opportunities. The importance of curiosity and the practice of lifelong learning will be explored. You'll stay adaptive in a world that is changing quickly if you embrace an attitude of constant exploration, and you'll also discover unexplored potential within yourself.

Although the path to adopting the Infinite Mindset is difficult, it carries the promise of opening the door to a future brimming with unending opportunities. Keep in mind that you can change your perspective and embrace the infinite as we go more into the chapters that come. It's time to start this life-changing journey and discover the limitless possibilities that lie ahead.

Chapter 2: Breaking Free from Limitations

The fundamental idea of the infinite mindset, which pushes us to welcome change, see obstacles as opportunities, and have faith in our limitless potential, was examined in the previous chapter. With this attitude in place, we can now focus on a vital phase of our journey: Breaking Free from Limitations.

Finding and Eliminating Self-Inflicted Barriers

There are many different types of limitations, but frequently the most difficult ones are the ones we place on ourselves. These limitations that we place on ourselves might become ingrained in our thinking, impeding our development and preventing us from realizing our full potential. The first step to accepting the infinite within us is recognizing and removing these obstacles.

Strategies to Overcome Fear and Self-Doubt .

Self-awareness is the first step in the path. We'll look at methods for identifying the limitations you may have placed on yourself. These obstacles may take the form of unfavorable self-talk, constrictive attitudes, or persistently influencing trauma from the past.

Challenging Limiting Beliefs: Limiting beliefs are among the most prevalent types of self-imposed constraints. We'll look at ways to refute and reinterpret these assumptions. You can do more and be more resilient if you replace self-doubt with self-belief.

Techniques for Combating Fear and Self-Doubt

Two of the major barriers to reaching our potential are fear and self-doubt. We can become paralyzed by them, unable to take chances or seize opportunities. We'll go into useful tactics to get over these barriers in this section.

The Use of Fear as a Catalyst: We'll discuss a mentality change that encourages you to perceive fear not as an impediment to growth but rather as a motivator for it. You can find the strength to venture outside of your comfort zone and take on new challenges by learning to dance with your fears.

Building Confidence: Lack of confidence is frequently the root of self-doubt. We'll examine methods for boosting and sustaining self-assurance, such as self-affirmation, visualization, and goal-setting. You'll learn that confidence is a talent that you can develop rather than a set quality.

Turning Obstacles into Opportunities

Obstacles are stepping stones rather than roadblocks in the journey towards accepting the infinite. By changing your attitude, you may turn setbacks into chances for development and innovation.

The Resilience Mindset: We'll talk about the resilience mindset, a way of thinking that encourages you to see challenges as chances to strengthen your resilience. You'll be better able to overcome obstacles in life if you can learn to recover from failures.

Adaptive Problem-Solving: Rather than viewing challenges as insurmountable barriers, we'll talk about adaptive problem-solving techniques. You'll discover how to take on obstacles with imagination and resourcefulness, using them as springboards for both your career and personal development.

As we proceed through this chapter, keep in mind that the process of overcoming restrictions is one that never ends. The mentality and abilities you acquire here are crucial for realizing your limitless potential as well as for building a life that is full of meaning, resiliency, and an endless desire for learning. It's time to throw off the chains of your restrictions and focus on an unrestricted future.

Chapter 3: The Creative Power of Limitlessness

The idea of limitlessness has a significant significance in the field of creativity. We can create, invent, and transform within the constraints of our imagination. This chapter focuses on the creative power of limitlessness, including how it fosters our creative potential, gives us tools to get beyond creative roadblocks, and enables us to access an unending supply of inspiration.

Nurturing Your Creative Potential

Although creativity is a natural human trait, it needs to be fostered and nurtured to grow. Limitlessness offers the best conditions for the development of creativity since it has limitless horizons.

The first step towards unleashing your inner creativity is to acknowledge that you already have it. Creativity is something that everyone possesses. We'll look at ways to unleash your creative side while utilizing your distinctive skills and viewpoints.

Adopting a Growth Mindset for Creativity: A growth mindset is equally important for creativity, as we mentioned in Chapter 1. You'll discover how to apply the growth mindset's principles to your creative endeavors, perceiving obstacles as chances for development and creativity.

Techniques to Overcome Creative Blocks

The enemies of unrestricted creativity are creative barriers, which frequently impede our growth. We'll provide you with some useful tips in this part to help you get beyond these challenges.

Understanding Creative Blockages: In this section, we'll examine the psychology of creative blockages to comprehend their causes and effects. You'll be more equipped to face and get over your particular obstacles if you can pinpoint them.

Unlocking the Creative Flow: The term "flow" refers to a state of intensely focused creativity. We'll look at ways to achieve this state, where time seems to stop, and creativity comes naturally. Some of the most amazing artistic creations are born in this state.

Tapping into Endless Inspiration

Inspiration knows no bounds in a world without boundaries. To support your creative endeavors, this section examines how to access a never-ending source of inspiration.

Developing an Observant Mind: Creative ideas frequently result from careful observation. We'll talk about how to develop an alert mind so that you can perceive the beauty and possibility in ordinary encounters.

Limitlessness offers us the chance to investigate various effects. We'll look at how ideas from several sectors can interact to produce ground-breaking innovation and creativity.

"As we dive deeper into Chapter 3, 'The Creative Power of Limitlessness,' let's explore how nurturing your creative potential, practicing mindfulness, embracing collaborative creativity, overcoming plateaus, engaging in creative exercises, and applying creativity in problem-solving can all converge to unlock a realm of limitless inspiration and innovation."

How to Move From Ideation to Execution in the Creative Process

Creativity is a disciplined process that anybody can learn to master; it is not a mysterious power reserved for a select few. The creative process will be deconstructed into essential stages in this part, along with tips on how to make the most of each stage.

- **Idea Generation:** The journey starts with an idea's glint. We'll examine methods for coming up with and honing ideas, including brainstorming sessions and finding inspiration from a variety of sources. You'll discover how to seize and develop your creative impulses.

- **Inspiration and Research:** Once you have a concept, it's time to do some inspiration and research. We'll talk about how to do research well, obtain pertinent data, and get ideas from a variety of places. Your creative effort becomes the foundation built on research.

- **Organisation and planning:** Structure fosters creativity. We'll go into detail about the significance of organizing and planning your creative work, from establishing specific objectives to defining schedules and milestones. You'll learn how organized preparation may stimulate your imagination.

- **Implementation and revision:** Now that your strategy is in place, it's time to put your creative vision into action. We'll talk about how to approach projects, deal with obstacles, and iterate on your work to make it better. The process of becoming creative frequently entails numerous draughts and modifications.

• **Collaboration and Feedback:** Creativity doesn't happen in a vacuum. We'll talk about the importance of input and teamwork in the creative process. You'll discover how to seek out constructive criticism, give it, and use the benefits of teamwork to improve your work.

• **Finishing and Celebrating:** The last step in the creative process entails finishing your creation and acknowledging your accomplishments. We'll talk about how to stay motivated and be proud of your artistic achievements.

The link between mindfulness and creativity is presence.

Practices that promote mindfulness are not only good for one's mental health but are also an effective way to boost creativity. This section will examine the significant relationship between mindfulness and creativity and offer insights into how practices like mindfulness and meditation can support people in developing their creative potential.

• **The Foundation of a Mindful Creative Mindset:** To start, let's lay the groundwork for a Mindful Creative Mindset. We'll talk about how mindfulness entails being present in the moment and how this presence can foster creativity. You'll discover how to use the present as a source of inspiration.

• **Meditation and Creative Insights:** Meditation is an inner-calming and clear-thinking practice. We'll explore how regular meditation might spur creative breakthroughs by reducing mental chatter and promoting the emergence of original ideas.

• **Mindful Observation:** Mindful observation is a crucial component of mindfulness. We'll look at how exercising acute awareness of your surroundings may inspire creativity. You'll learn how unassuming features and commonplace events can serve as sources of creative inspiration.

• **Accepting Ambiguity:** Mindfulness teaches us to accept ambiguity and uncertainty. We'll talk about how being willing to spend time in the dark can unleash your creativity from the confines of dogmatic thinking. You'll discover how to embrace uncertainty as a space for imaginative experimentation.

• **Mindfulness and Problem Solving:** In addition to artistic endeavors, problem-solving can benefit greatly from the use of mindfulness. We'll talk about how practicing mindfulness can improve your capacity to face obstacles, make informed choices, and come up with original solutions.

• **Mindful Creativity in Practice:** We'll offer activities and approaches that readers may implement into their everyday routines to put mindfulness into practice. You may use the power of mindfulness to unleash your creative potential with the aid of these exercises.

Collaboration and Creativity: Opening Up New Horizons

Although solo innovation is amazing, working together has tremendous power. We will highlight the transformative power of collaborative creativity in this part and offer suggestions for successful teamwork and idea generation.

• **The Synergy of Collaboration:** In this section, we'll discuss the idea of synergy, which holds that a group's combined creative efforts can vastly outweigh individual contributions. You'll comprehend why teamwork catalyzes creative thoughts.

• **Effective Communication:** Effective communication is a prerequisite for effective teamwork. We'll talk about techniques for effective and frank communication within a creative team. You'll discover how to communicate your thoughts, offer criticism, and promote teamwork.

• **Diverse Perspectives:** The variety of perspectives that collaboration fosters is one of its advantages. We'll stress the value of welcoming individuals with various perspectives and life experiences into a creative team. You'll learn how this diversity can result in more complex and creative solutions.

• **Idea Generation in Teams:** The process of generating ideas collaboratively can be dynamic. We'll offer methods for idea-generating and brainstorming in a group setting. You'll discover how to tap into your group's collective creativity.

• **Conflict Resolution:** Conflicts can arise in collaborative projects. We'll discuss dispute resolution tactics, with a focus on the value of productive communication and compromise. You'll learn techniques for handling conflicts in a way that encourages creativity rather than stifles it.

• **Case Studies in Collaboration:** We'll present actual case studies of fruitful collaborations to highlight the power of collaborative innovation.

These examples will show how teamwork can produce truly inventive results.

Reviving the Creative Spark After a Creative Block

Every creative process has plateaus—times when inspiration is difficult to come by. In this section, we'll discuss methods for getting over creative ruts, maintaining motivation, and reviving your inspiration when it seems to have dried up.

• **Recognising Creative Plateaus:** In this section, we'll talk about how to spot indicators of a creative plateau including dissatisfaction, boredom, or creative burnout. You'll discover how to recognize a creative block.

• **Thinking shifts:** Breaking through a plateau frequently calls for a thinking change. We'll look at methods for changing your viewpoint and reframing difficulties as chances for development. You'll learn how to see plateaus as a natural part of the creative process.

• **Leaving Your Comfort Zone:** When you leave your comfort zone, creativity can sometimes flourish. We'll talk about how important it is to try new things and take chances. You'll discover how to add a dash of uniqueness to your artistic endeavors.

• **Discovering New Inspirational Sources:** When inspiration wanes, it's time to look for fresh inspiration. We'll offer tips for finding new sources of inspiration, from taking up new activities to connecting with other artistic mediums.

• **Creative Rituals:** By giving structure and habit, developing creative rituals can help you get past plateaus. We'll give you some ideas for creative rituals and help you come up with your own. You'll establish routines that inspire new creative ideas.

• **Community and Support:** Surrounding oneself with other creative people can help you get over slumps and stay motivated. We'll talk about the advantages of finding mentors or participating in creative organizations. You'll learn how connecting with others may inspire your creativity.

Exercises and Prompts to Spark Creativity and Innovation

When you actively participate in creativity, it flourishes. We'll provide a range of creative exercises and suggestions in this section that readers may use to spark their imaginations, get beyond writer's block, or break through creative blocks. These activities are intended to spark your creativity and promote a fun mindset.

- **Freewriting and Stream of Consciousness:** In this section, we'll discuss the idea of freewriting, a method in which you write without restraint or self-censorship. You'll discover how this technique enables you to access your subconscious and unearth buried concepts.

- **Visual journaling:** To inspire creativity, visual journaling blends words and images. We'll give instructions on how to make a visual journal so you can use it to express yourself and explore your creativity.

- **Creative Prompts:** We'll provide a variety of prompts for writing, visual arts, and music, as well as other forms of expression. You can use these questions as a jumping-off point for your creative projects.

- **Collage and Mixed Media:** You can experiment with different materials and textures when creating collage and mixed media artwork. We'll look at how these tactile creative expressions can spark new concepts and broaden your creative boundaries.

• **Creative Challenges:** Put yourself to the test with time-bound creative activities. We'll give you tasks that push you to act swiftly and believe in your gut. You'll learn how limitations can stimulate creativity.

• **Storytelling Exercises:** A fundamental form of creativity is storytelling. You can create characters, plotlines, and tales with the help of the storytelling activities we'll provide. You'll discover that narrative is a flexible tool for creativity.

Problem-solving Creativity: Moving Beyond the Limits of the Arts

Creativity is a powerful tool for problem-solving in many facets of life, including business, personal development, and innovation. It is not just limited to the fields of art and expression. This section will look at how creativity may be used to solve a variety of problems and cross the boundaries of the arts.

• **Creative Problem-Solving Frameworks:** We'll discuss creative problem-solving frameworks including the SCAMPER method and Design Thinking. You'll discover how to use these techniques to tackle problems in the real world.

• **Creativity in Business:** In the business world, creativity drives innovation. We'll talk about how companies use innovation to create novel goods, services, and business models. You'll get tips on how to promote an innovative culture.

• **Creativity and Personal Development:** Creativity can be a tool for development and self-discovery. We'll look at how artistic expression and other creative activities can support human growth.

• **Education and Creativity:** Education and creativity go hand in hand. We'll talk about how teachers can encourage students' creativity while also developing their critical thinking and problem-solving abilities. You'll learn how creativity improves education.

• **Creativity and Innovation:** Innovation frequently results from imaginative thought. We'll explore how the creative process results in novel solutions. You'll comprehend the connection between innovation and advancement better.

• **Creativity and Leadership:** To promote change and innovation inside organizations, creative leadership is a potent force. We'll talk about the use of creativity by leaders to motivate and direct their teams to success.

Risk-taking and Creativity: Embracing the Unknown

Taking risks is a crucial component of the creative process. In this section, we'll examine the connection between creativity and taking calculated risks, highlighting the value of doing so to foster creativity.

• **Creativity as a Leap of Faith:** Being creative frequently entails taking risks and venturing into the uncharted. We'll talk about having the guts to welcome uncertainty and take calculated risks. You'll discover how to follow your creative dreams and believe in your gut.

• **Fear of Failure:** Being afraid of failing can be a major deterrent to taking creative risks. We'll look at ways to get over this anxiety and reframe failure as a beneficial learning opportunity. You'll learn that the creative process includes failure as a necessary step.

• **Breaking customs:** When you question norms and customs, creativity flourishes. We'll talk about how to challenge conventional wisdom and think creatively. You'll discover how to welcome nonconformity as an inspiration for innovation.

- **Experimenting and iterating:** Taking risks frequently entails experimenting and iterating. We'll explore how making mistakes can spark original ideas. You'll develop a willingness to accept experimentation as a means of learning.

- **Honouring Creative Risk-Taking**: Honouring creative risk-taking is important regardless of the result. We'll talk about how critical it is to value and appreciate your creative endeavors, especially when they diverge from the norm.

- **Role Models for Risk-Taking:** We'll give instances of people and organizations who have taken big risks and experienced amazing creative achievement. You'll be motivated to explore unexplored creative waters by these tales.

Case Studies: Insights from Unbound Creativity

We'll share case studies of people and organizations that have effectively used creative power to produce exceptional results to demonstrate the transformative potential of boundless creativity. The insights learned from these real-world instances can help you on your creative journey.

- **Technological Innovations:** We'll look at how tech behemoths like Apple and Google have transformed entire industries with ground-breaking inventions. You'll discover how their success was largely attributed to their capacity for innovation and risk-taking.

• **Creative Works of Art:** The art world is full of examples of artists who pushed boundaries and questioned norms. We'll talk about well-known artists like Pablo Picasso and Frida Kahlo and look at how their inventiveness changed the face of art.

• **Entrepreneurial Success Stories:** Creativity and entrepreneurship frequently go hand in hand. We'll highlight business owners who successfully turned their concepts into profitable ventures while highlighting the importance of creativity in their development.

• **Scientific Breakthroughs:** Innovative thinking and problem-solving lead to scientific discoveries. We'll look at the lives of famous scientists like Marie Curie and Albert Einstein and emphasize their innovative solutions to difficult problems.

• **Social Change Movements:** In social change movements, creativity is crucial. Examining how innovation fuelled activism and change, we'll look at movements like the Women's Suffrage Movement and the Civil Rights Movement.

• **Personal Transformation:** Accounts from real people who have changed themselves through creativity. These tales will demonstrate how creativity can be a tool for personal development.

Building Creative Habits: Promoting Consistency

Creativity's foundation is consistency. This section will offer advice on how to develop and maintain daily creative habits so that creativity becomes a regular and essential part of your routine.

• **The Power of Routine:** We'll talk about how routine may provide creative endeavors shape and stability. Daily routines will teach you how to foster a creatively stimulating environment.

• Setting clear goals is the first step in creating effective creative habits. Whatever your creative goals are—whether they entail writing, art, or another form of expression—we'll talk about how to define and prioritize them.

• **Accountability and tracking:** Keeping your creative habits in check requires holding yourself accountable. We'll talk about methods for keeping tabs on your creative development and resolving to pursue your creative objectives.

• **Establishing a Creative Space:** Having a designated space for creation might encourage it. We'll offer advice on how to set up and decorate a setting that stimulates your inventiveness. You'll discover how to foster an environment that encourages invention.

• **Morning routines:** Establishing creative habits frequently starts with morning rituals. We'll give examples of morning routines that get the day started right and inspire creativity.

• **Overcoming Procrastination:** It might hinder the development of creative habits. We'll look at methods for avoiding procrastination and maintaining concentration on your artistic endeavors. You'll learn methods for creative productivity.

Structure and Freedom in Balance: The Art of Creative Coherence

Within the creative process, striking a careful balance between order and freedom is difficult. We'll talk about how striking the ideal balance between structure and flexibility may foster creativity in this part.

• **The Creative Tension:** In this section, we'll examine how the interaction of structure and freedom can produce creative tension, which acts as a catalyst for the advancement of your work. You'll discover how to use this tension to spark original thought.

• **Establishing a Framework:** A framework for creativity is provided by structure. We'll talk about how to construct an adaptable framework that supports your creative endeavors without restricting spontaneity. You'll locate a balance that complements your artistic approach.

The advantages and disadvantages of routines and spontaneity in the creative process will be discussed. You'll learn when to stick to a schedule and when to value spontaneity.

• **Creative Constraints:** By promoting creative thinking, constraints can improve creativity. We'll look at how to create limitations that promote problem-solving and creativity.

• **Inspiration and Structure:** Inspiration can come from structure. We'll talk about how structure can direct your creative exploration so you can explore your creative ideas more thoroughly.

- **Flexibility and Adaptability:** Success in the creative process depends on one's capacity to adjust to shifting conditions. We'll offer techniques for maintaining adaptability and dealing with unforeseen creative difficulties.

The Function of Failure in Creativity: Accepting Development

Failure is a stepping stone to growth and invention, not the end of creativity. In this section, we'll stress how failure is a normal part of the creative process and how it can result in important realizations and innovations.

- **The Fear of Failure:** We'll talk about how creativity might be hampered by the fear of failure. You'll develop the ability to identify this fear and deal with it head-on while realizing that it's a typical experience of the creative process.

- **Reframing Failure:** Rather than seeing failure as a setback, we'll look at techniques for reinterpreting it as a priceless learning opportunity. Gaining these skills will help you learn from mistakes and apply those lessons to your future artistic endeavors.

• **Creative Resilience:** The capacity to recover from setbacks is resilience. We'll talk about the idea of creative resilience, focusing on how it helps you endure in the face of obstacles to creativity.

• **Failure as a Catalyst for Innovation:** In this section, we'll give examples of how failure has sparked innovation in a variety of sectors. You'll get an understanding of how failure may result in novel, ground-breaking creative solutions.

• **Accepting Failure:** Since exploration by its very nature contains the prospect of failure, creativity frequently involves it. You'll be urged to embrace experimenting as a way to expand your creative horizons.

• **Case Studies in Creative Resilience:** Actual cases of people and organizations who overcame obstacles in their creative endeavors and became stronger. You will be motivated by these case studies to see failure as a springboard for reaching greater creative heights.

Using Creative Visualisation to Make Your Vision Real

A potent method for achieving your creative objectives is creative visualization. We'll discuss creative visualization strategies in this section to assist readers in clearly imagining and realizing their creative visions.

• **The Art of Creative Visualisation:** In this section, we'll discuss the idea of using creative visualization as a method to tap into the creative force of the mind. You'll comprehend how visualization helps ideas become reality.

• **Guided Visualisation Exercises:** We'll provide you with exercises that will help you explore your imaginative visions. You can use these exercises to access the sensory components of your creative thoughts.

• **Visualisation for Goal Achievement:** Setting and attaining creative goals can be aided through creative visualization. We'll talk about using visualization to picture your creative success and take concrete steps in that direction.

• Mood boards are visual representations of imaginative concepts. We'll look at how to make inspiration-filled mood boards that encapsulate the core of your artistic vision.

• Visual diaries and vision journals are both places to record and develop your creative ideas. As a tool for creative visualization, we'll walk you through the process of developing your vision notebook.

• **The Mind-Body Connection:** Visualisation involves both the body and the mind. We'll talk about how the mind-body link affects your actions and results when you visualize creatively.

Long-Term Creativity Maintenance: A Strenuous Journey

Long-term creativity maintenance is a rewarding but difficult endeavor. This section will include methods for preserving creativity, avoiding burnout, and preserving passion for creative endeavors.

• **The Creative Marathon:** Being creative is a marathon, not a sprint. We'll emphasize how critical it is to approach your creative path with a long-term perspective. You'll develop the stamina to persevere in the face of imaginative difficulties.

Avoiding Burnout: Burnout can impede creativity. We'll talk about how to avoid burnout and keep a positive work-life-creativity balance. You'll gain knowledge about the warning signs of burnout and how to prevent it.

• **Rest and recovery:** For continuous creativity, rest and recovery are crucial. We'll look at how rest can inspire new ideas. You'll learn the significance of relaxation as a catalyst for creativity.

Setting creative milestones can inspire you and give you a sense of accomplishment. We'll talk about how to create creative milestones that divide more complex tasks into doable steps. You'll continue to feel forward motion.

• **Creative retreats:** These facilities provide a focused period and place for creative endeavors. We'll look at how to organize and go on creative retreats that offer a fresh perspective and a boost of inspiration.

• **Adapting to Changing Interests:** Over time, your creative interests may change. We'll talk about how to adjust to these changes and still be creative. You'll discover how to welcome the natural progression of your creativity.

Chapter 4: Career Development and Endless Possibilities

Our careers are a crucial setting where we can apply these ideas to attain outstanding achievement as we seek to unlock infinity and embrace limitless possibilities. The discussion of career advancement, meaningful connections, and achieving professional success with purpose is the focus of Chapter 4.

Strategies for Advancing Your Career

Success in a profession involves more than just moving up the corporate ladder; it also involves constant improvement, the acquisition of new skills, and a sense of fulfillment. We will explore a variety of tactics that can advance your career in this part.

Why Creating Ambitious Goals: Progress is fueled by ambition. We'll talk about the value of establishing lofty professional aspirations that push you to broaden your horizons and shoot for the stars. You'll discover how to match your objectives with your long-term objectives.

• **Constant learning and skill improvement:** Strive for excellence always. We'll look at how adopting a growth mindset and spending money on ongoing education can help you develop new talents and stay on the cutting edge of your industry.

• **efficient Time Management:** Although time is a limited resource, you may increase your productivity and accomplish more in less time by using efficient time management. We'll offer doable tactics for setting priorities and reducing distractions.

• **Coaching and mentoring:** The advice provided by coaches and mentors can be priceless. We'll go over ways to locate mentors who can offer guidance, counsel, and support as you advance in your profession.

• **Personal branding:** Your identity as a professional is reflected in your brand. We'll discuss the idea of personal branding and how to build a potent, genuine brand that distinguishes you in your field.

• **Adaptability and Resilience:** In a world that is changing quickly, these qualities are essential. We'll talk about how to accept change, recover from failures, and see problems as chances for development.

• **Strategic Risk-Taking:** Carefully considered risks can result in substantial benefits. We'll explore the art of taking calculated risks, guiding you in recognizing possibilities worth pursuing and evaluating possible consequences.

Networking and Building Meaningful Connections

Your value is in your network. It's not only a professional tactic to establish meaningful connections; doing so opens up a world of possibilities. We will discuss the art of networking and cultivating real connections in this part.

- The Power of Networking: Building real relationships through networking goes beyond simply exchanging business cards. We'll talk about networking's revolutionary power and how to do it honestly.

- Strategies for Effective Networking: Networking takes planning and strategy. We'll offer helpful advice on how to network successfully at conferences, events, and within your current professional networks.

- Social media and internet networking are equally important in the current digital era. We'll show you how to leverage the power of social media websites and online forums to grow your network.

- Creating Meaningful Connections: Meaningful relationships go beyond cursory interactions. We'll look at how to create connections based on mutual respect, trust, and values.

- Mentoring is a two-way street; both giving and receiving mentoring. We'll talk about the advantages of both offering and receiving mentoring for personal development.

- Networking with a Purpose: Effective networking is motivated by a purpose rather than being random. We'll assist you in defining your networking objectives and customizing your efforts to suit your professional goals.

Achieving Professional Success with Purpose

Real professional success goes beyond achievement; it's about giving your work meaning and a purpose. We will explore the significant relationship between achievement and meaning in this part.

- Identifying Your Professional Purpose: Your career journey is guided by your professional purpose. You can match your actions with your inner values and objectives by discovering your professional purpose with our assistance.

- Striking a balance between ambition and fulfillment: While pursuing success is admirable, it shouldn't come at the expense of happiness. We'll talk about finding a happy medium between ambition and a sense of fulfillment motivated by a purpose.

- Influential Leadership: Influence and impact are more important than mere position when it comes to leadership. We'll talk about the characteristics of effective leadership and how to inspire those around you by leading with purpose.

- Corporate Social Responsibility (CSR): The most prosperous organizations understand the significance of CSR. We'll talk about how you may support the mission-driven efforts of your company and improve society.

- Measuring Success Beyond Metrics: Metrics and KPIs are not the only ways to measure success. We'll question accepted ideas of success and prod you to think about the bigger picture of how your work affects your neighborhood and the rest of the globe.

- Work-Life Integration: Harmony between work and life is necessary for success with a purpose. We'll look at methods for balancing your career goals with a happy personal life.

Your road map to a fruitful and rewarding profession is found in Chapter 4. A profound feeling of purpose in your professional endeavors, strategic career progression, and genuine networking are all part of the journey. You'll discover that success takes on a deeper and more meaningful dimension as you delve into these tactics and ideas, pointing you in the direction of an endless universe of employment prospects.

Establishing a Personal Advisory Board to Help You Manage Your Career

The value of seeking advice and mentoring cannot be emphasized in the constantly changing professional environment. This section examines the idea of assembling a personal advisory board—a knowledgeable group of people who may offer crucial advice and guidance throughout your career journey.

The Importance of a Personal Advisory Board

We have access to a wealth of information in the digital age, but wisdom is frequently found in the advice of knowledgeable mentors. Learn why creating a personal advisory board is a wise career decision.

Choosing the Best Consultants:

A crucial stage is selecting the members of your advisory board. Learn to spot people that fit your career goals in terms of knowledge, experience, and values.

Diverse Viewpoints for Holistic Development:

Your advisory board's diversity fosters a range of viewpoints. Examine how advisors with diverse experiences and expertise in different fields might enlarge your perspective.

Fostering Relationships with Mentors:

It takes skill to develop solid mentorship bonds. Learn how to build trusting relationships with your advisors and use their knowledge to your advantage.

Having Good Communication Skills is Essential for Career Advancement:

Effective communication skills are essential in the connected and hectic workplace of today. The importance of developing your communication skills—both verbal and written, active listening, and the ability to persuade and influence others—is emphasized in this section.

The Influence of Good Communication:

Find out why successful interpersonal and organizational dynamics depend on effective communication.

Mastery of Written Communication:

Examine the subtleties of written communication, including how to write effective emails, reports, and documents.

Developing Verbal Communication Skills:

Effective verbal communication involves more than just words; it also involves presence, tone, and body language. Learn how to perform well in conversations, meetings, and presentations.

The Lost Art of Active Listening:

Active listening is a talent that is sometimes undervalued but is crucial for creating teamwork and trust. Explore methods for becoming a focused and sympathetic listener.

The Science of Influence and Persuasion:

Influence is a potent instrument for professional development. Learn techniques for ethically and successfully influencing others.

Negotiation and Conflict Resolution: Succeeding Despite Obstacles:

Professional disagreement is inevitable, so developing negotiating and conflict resolution skills are essential for career advancement. This section offers doable tactics for successfully negotiating and settling disputes.

Understanding the Dynamics of Conflict:

Learn more about the types of disputes that arise in the workplace and how those conflicts may affect your career path.

Conflict Management Techniques:

Investigate tried-and-true methods for resolving disputes that can assist you in negotiating difficult situations with coworkers, supervisors, or clients.

A Negotiation's Art:

The ability to negotiate can increase your earning potential and help you develop in your job. Learn effective bargaining techniques to get successful results.

Win-Win Approach to Negotiation:

Learn about the win-win negotiation strategy, which focuses on developing friendly relationships and finding solutions that benefit both parties.

Managing Your Digital Reputation: Creating a Strong Online Presence

Your internet presence is crucial in today's digital age for establishing your professional brand. This section discusses the value of controlling your online reputation and offers advice on how to keep a respectable and positive online presence.

How Important Digital Reputation Is

Recognize how employer perceptions, job chances, and personal branding may be impacted by your internet presence.

How to Create and Manage Your Online Presence:

Learn how to build and maintain a professional online presence that supports your career objectives and showcases your professional competence.

Etiquette and Best Practises for Social Media:

Learn the dos and don'ts of using social media for business, as well as techniques for networking and developing a solid online reputation.

Online Security and Privacy:

Protecting your online identity is essential. Learn how to safeguard your personal and professional information online.

How to handle offensive online content:

Develop techniques for managing and reducing the impact of negative online content on your reputation as you face the challenges of dealing with it.

Creating Your Online Personal Brand: Your Digital Identity

Personal branding expands into the digital sphere in addition to the physical one. The information in this part will help you develop and market your brand on multiple websites.

Personal and professional branding in conjunction

Recognize the relationship between your personal and professional brands and how it affects your ability to succeed in your job.

Using LinkedIn to Advance Your Career

Building your professional presence online can be accomplished with the help of LinkedIn. Examine methods for enhancing your LinkedIn profile and productively communicating with your network.

How to Build a Personal Website

Discover the advantages of using a personal website as a platform to highlight your knowledge, successes, and portfolio.

Social Media Techniques for Building Personal Brands

Learn how to strategically use social media platforms for your brand, including advice on content production, audience development, and engagement.

Global Networking: Increasing Possibilities and Horizons

The world is more connected than ever, and international networking opens doors to a wide range of viewpoints and unending employment chances. The importance of broadening your professional network beyond local or regional limits is highlighted in this section.

The Benefits of a World Network

Investigate the advantages of networking with businesspeople from different countries, such as exposure to fresh perspectives and business chances.

Online Resources for Global Networking

Learn about Internet resources that enhance global networking and make it simpler to connect with experts.

Cultural Sensitivity in International Networking

Building international relationships requires navigating cultural differences. Discover how to build cultural competence and steer clear of frequent mistakes.

Cross-border communication that works

Global communication requires cultural awareness to be effective. Explore methods for corresponding and working with overseas partners.

Your Path to Innovation Through Entrepreneurship and Intrapreneurship

Career advancement and innovation are possible through entrepreneurship and intrapreneurship. These ideas, their variations, and their possibilities for advancing a creative career are examined in this section.

Entrepreneurship and Intrapreneurship Definition

Explain what it means to be an entrepreneur (creating your firm) and an intrapreneur (using innovative thinking within a company), as well as the special opportunities they each offer.

How to Navigate the Startup Journey in Entrepreneurship

Discover the steps involved in starting a successful business, from brainstorming and developing a business to launching and scaling it.

Fostering Innovation Within Organisations Through Intrapreneurship

Learn how intrapreneurship may promote innovation, address organizational issues, and advance your career within a current company.

Entrepreneurship and Intrapreneurship: Balancing Risk and Reward

Determine the rewards and dangers of entrepreneurship and intrapreneurship, and then devise a tactical plan for minimizing dangers and maximizing opportunities.

Making Moral Decisions: Maintaining Integrity in Your Career

A responsible and rewarding career is built on the foundation of ethical decision-making. The significance of ethical factors, values, and integrity in career decisions is covered in this section.

Ethics' Place in Career Advancement

Recognize the importance of ethical decision-making for long-term professional success and personal fulfillment.

Managing Ethical Conundrums

Examine practical ethical conundrums that professionals may face in their jobs as well as decision-making techniques.

Integrity as an Asset for Personal Branding

Integrity is an important facet of your brand. Learn how upholding moral principles can help you build a solid professional reputation.

Having a healthy mind and emotional stability is essential for success.

The ability to succeed in your profession is inextricably related to your mental and emotional health. The significance of preserving one's mental and emotional well-being, controlling stress, and striking a work-life balance are all discussed in this section.

Career Performance and Mental and Emotional Well-Being

Be aware of the link between mental and emotional health and career performance, including output, judgment, and interpersonal interactions.

Techniques for Stress Reduction

Examine useful practices, such as mindfulness practices and relaxation exercises, for reducing stress in demanding professional settings.

Making Work-Life Balance Work

To sustain a profession over the long term, it is crucial to maintain a healthy work-life balance. Learn how to strike a balance between your personal and professional goals.

Success in the Workplace and Emotional Intelligence

Learn how to improve your emotional intelligence and how it plays a role in leadership, communication, and professional relationships.

Your Road to Relevance: Lifelong Learning and Development

In a competitive employment market, lifelong learning and ongoing professional development are essential for staying relevant and competitive. This section offers information on tools, programs, and continuous learning tactics.

The Need for Lifelong Education

Learn why lifelong learning is important in today's ever-evolving job market and how it advances careers.

Opportunities for Formal and Informal Learning

Learn about several opportunities for informal learning, including books, podcasts, and online courses, as well as official schooling and certificates.

Construction of a Personal Learning Plan

Create a personalized learning plan that is in line with your professional aspirations, interests, and areas of interest.

Keeping Current and Being Flexible

Learn how to keep up with market developments, industry trends, and emerging technology to stay flexible and responsive to change.

Career Alignment with Purpose in Sustainability and Corporate Social Responsibility (CSR)

CSR and sustainability are essential elements of ethical business practices. This section looks at how professionals can support sustainability initiatives inside their companies and match their jobs with moral and ethical behavior.

The Function of Experts in Sustainability

Recognize the different ways that people in all jobs and industries may support sustainability projects and have a positive influence.

Sustainability Integration into Business Practises

Learn about methods for incorporating sustainability into company practices, including supply chain management, product creation, and marketing.

As a Career Catalyst, CSR

Learn how adopting CSR can improve your workplace satisfaction, career possibilities, and alignment with a larger sense of purpose.

Making a Personal Mission Statement: Using It to Guide Your Career

Your life and work decisions should be guided by your mission statement. This section challenges readers to develop personal mission statements that encompass their values, aspirations, and professional objectives.

The Career Driven by Purpose

Recognize the enormous effects of guiding your job decisions with a strong sense of meaning and purpose.

Personal Mission Statement Creation

step-by-step instructions for writing a personal mission statement that encapsulates your basic beliefs, aspirations, and values.

Using Your Career Compass to Follow Your Mission Statement

Discover how to use your mission statement to determine priorities, handle professional hurdles, and make wise career decisions.

Integrating Diversity and Inclusion to Promote Growth

Not only are diversity and inclusion moral requirements, but they also spur creativity and development. This section looks at the advantages of workplace diversity and how to create welcoming environments.

The Case for Diversity in Business

Examine the persuasive arguments for why businesses benefit from prioritizing diversity and inclusion, such as improved creativity and competitiveness.

The Case for Diversity in the Workplace: Increasing Organisational Excellence

Diversity and inclusion have evolved beyond being trendy buzzwords in today's fast-paced, globally connected corporate environment to become critical factors in an organization's success. Businesses that value diversity and foster inclusive cultures profit in numerous ways that go far beyond upholding their moral and social obligations. In this section, we'll look at some of the strong arguments for why businesses should prioritize diversity and inclusion in their plans if they want to succeed

Promoting innovation and creativity

The introduction of new viewpoints and ideas is one of the workforce's most important benefits. The potential for creativity and invention soars when people from various backgrounds, experiences, and cultures join together. Diverse teams tackle issues from various perspectives, resulting in ground-breaking solutions and unconventional thinking. When people are encouraged to contribute their distinctive ideas, creativity abounds. This creativity fuels innovation, propels the development of new products, and distinguishes businesses in a cutthroat market.

Increasing Competition

Diversity is a competitive advantage that goes beyond political correctness. Companies that support diversity benefit from a competitive advantage by accessing a larger talent pool. As more people look for jobs that promote diversity and offer inclusive workplaces, this competitive advantage also applies to luring and keeping great talent. A varied workforce mirrors the diversity of the consumer base in many industries, assisting businesses in better comprehending and meeting the needs of their customers. Additionally, it encourages the development of global viewpoints, which are crucial for businesses competing in today's global marketplaces.

Increasing Market Coverage

An organization's diversity mirrors the diversity of the markets it serves. When a company's workforce reflects its clientele, it is better able to establish relationships with a broad spectrum of clients. In marketing and sales, being aware of the cultural quirks, tastes, and demands of different demographic groups can make all the difference. Along with strengthening client ties, it also makes room for new markets and sources of income. Businesses that value diversity are better able to cater their goods and services to a variety of markets, thereby growing their influence and reach.

Making Better Decisions

Teams with a variety of members are more likely to make educated decisions. Multiple viewpoints enable a more thorough analysis of difficult problems. When people from various backgrounds and perspectives work together to analyze possibilities, they challenge presumptions, reduce prejudices, and make more rational and sensible choices. In today's complicated and quickly changing corporate world, when adaptation and agility are crucial, this collaborative decision-making process is especially valuable.

Increasing Employee Loyalty and Engagement

Employees feel more valued and at home in a diverse and welcoming workplace. People are more likely to be involved in and devoted to their positions when they feel that their distinctive identities and contributions are valued. High employee engagement also contributes to lower turnover and higher productivity. Employee loyalty increases with respect and inclusion, which promotes an organization's long-term stability and success.

Risk reduction for the law and reputation

Organizations can steer clear of risky legal and public relations situations by proactively embracing diversity and inclusion. Raising awareness of fairness and equality through non-discriminatory policies and inclusive practices lowers the likelihood of discrimination litigation. Additionally, organizations that are viewed as diversity champions are positively perceived by the public, which can improve brand reputation and consumer trust.

Conclusion

Diversity in the workplace has a strong financial justification as well as moral and strategic reasons. Diverse and inclusive workplaces are better positioned for long-term success, innovation, and greatness. They are better able to deal with the complexity of the contemporary corporate environment, access a variety of markets, and promote a creative, collaborative, and adaptable culture. They succeed by embracing diversity and making use of its enormous potential to propel success.

Organizations may harness the boundless potential that varied and inclusive environments provide, ultimately achieving greatness in the global marketplace, by comprehending and embracing the strong business case for diversity.

Chapter 5: Building an Infinite Future

It's essential to apply these concepts outside of our professions and into the bigger picture of life in our quest to unlock infinity and embrace limitless possibilities. In Chapter 5, "Building an Infinite Future," the author discusses how to create lofty goals for one's life, make long-term plans for success, and maintain resilience in the face of difficulties.

Setting Ambitious Life Goals

Ambition encompasses the vast fabric of our lives and is not limited to our professional pursuits. This section examines the transforming potential of establishing lofty life objectives that motivate us to aim for the stars.

Life Goals and Their Influence

Learn why having big life goals is essential to living a satisfying and purposeful life. Life objectives provide people with meaning, motivation, and direction.

Setting a Goal for Your Life

Setting meaningful goals begins with creating a compelling life vision. We will assist you in determining the goals and purpose of your life.

Goal-Setting Techniques

Learn how to develop objectives that are specific, measurable, achievable, relevant, and time-bound (SMART) and how to use visualization to your advantage.

Keeping Long-Term and Short-Term Goals in Balance

Learn how to reconcile short-term needs with long-term aspirations so that your objectives line up with your overall life vision.

Creating a Long-Term Success Plan

The key to long-term success is strategic planning and constant commitment, not just wishful thinking. This section delves into the skill of making plans for a successful and fulfilling future.

Planning Your Life

Learn the importance of developing a thorough life plan that details your objectives, tactics, and checkpoints at various life stages.

Putting Financial Planning Into Practise

Long-term success is fundamentally dependent on financial security. We'll look at methods for budgeting, investing, saving, and planning for retirement.

Personal Development and Growth

Your quest for personal development is a lifelong endeavor. Learn how to continually improve your abilities, knowledge, and character traits to succeed in the long run.

Staying Resilient in the Face of Challenges

Maintaining Resilience Despite Obstacles

Life is full of obstacles, and resilience is the secret to getting through them. In this section, we explore the foundations of resilience and methods for overcoming the challenges that come with life.

Recognizing Resilience

Explore the idea of resilience and discover why it's so important for overcoming obstacles, misfortune, and unforeseen life occurrences.

Strategies for Building Resilience

Examine doable strategies for enhancing resilience, such as mindfulness, optimistic thinking, emotional quotient, and getting assistance when required.

Understanding Change

Change is a given in a dynamic life. Learn to embrace change as a chance for progress as you go through life's transformations.

Tenacity and Grit

Learn how tenacity and persistence can help you achieve your goals in life. Resilience and long-term success are founded on these traits.

Final Thoughts: Creating an Infinite Future

Chapter 5 leads you on a quest to create an endless future that is full of ambition, purpose, and unshakeable resiliency. You can seize the limitless chances that lie ahead of you by developing the resilience to deal with life's adversities, setting high standards for yourself, and making long-term strategic plans. Your voyage into an infinite future is a testimonial to a life well lived, not just a reflection of your professional accomplishment.

Chapter 6: Technology and Innovation in the Infinite Age

Innovation and technology act as strong catalysts for individual development and endless potential in the age of limitless possibility. You are invited to read Chapter 6, "Innovation and Technology in the Infinite Age," to learn more about the relationship between innovation and personal growth, to embrace new technology, and to appreciate the crucial place that innovation plays in your life.

Exploring the Intersection of Innovation and Personal Growth

Innovation has a significant impact on our personal growth and development and is not just relevant to business and industry. We explore the mutually beneficial relationship between innovation and the development of human potential in this section.

The Role of Innovation in Personal Development

Learn how innovation affects our lives, advances society, and gives us the resources and possibilities for lifelong improvement.

Innovation and Creativity in Personal Development

Learn how to use innovation to improve your abilities and explore the creative processes that support personal development.

An attitude of innovative thinking

Innovative thinking is a technique of looking at problems and opportunities. Learn how to foster imaginative thinking to successfully negotiate the challenges of life.

Embracing Emerging Technologies

Technology offers unheard-of opportunities for personal development as it develops at an exponential rate. This section encourages you to accept new technology and use it to broaden your perspective.

Technology Is Advancing Quickly

Learn about the ramifications of technology's amazing rate of advancement for daily living and personal growth.

Examining New Technologies

Explore the world of cutting-edge technologies, such as biotechnology, blockchain, virtual reality, and artificial intelligence, and learn how they might affect your path.

The Role of Innovation in Your Personal Journey

Learn about a variety of technological platforms, apps, and tools that can help with personal growth, such as productivity apps, mindfulness apps, and e-learning platforms.

Innovation's Place in Your Journey

Innovation serves as a catalyst for our journeys, not just as a tool. This section examines how innovation directs our lives, advances us, and makes it possible for us to realize our goals.

Innovation as a Change Catalyst

Discover true tales of people who have used creativity to reinvent themselves, get over obstacles, and accomplish their goals.

Individual Innovation Techniques

Learn how to use cutting-edge tactics in your journey, from establishing bold objectives for yourself to trying out novel solutions.

New Technology and Lifelong Learning

Learn how innovation and ongoing education work together to keep you adaptive and current in a world that is constantly changing.

The Inspirational Power of Innovation

Learn how innovation may inspire enthusiasm, creativity, and a desire to push the limits of what you thought were possible in your quest for personal development.

Conclusion: Progressing in the Infinite Age

Technology and invention are dynamic forces that influence our lives and enable us to aspire for the infinite, as Chapter 6 reminds us. They are not just tools. You can navigate the endless opportunities of the infinite age and map a path toward a future defined by innovation, personal growth, and limitless potential by understanding the profound relationship between innovation and personal growth, embracing emerging technologies, and adopting innovative thinking as a mindset.

Chapter 7: Spiritual Awakening and Internal Contentment

We enter into the spiritual world on the path to the unlocked infinite, where profound realizations and inner fulfillment await. In Chapter 7, "Spiritual Enlightenment and Inner Fulfilment," the author examines the search for spiritual purpose, the healing potential of mindfulness and meditation techniques, and the skill of achieving harmony and balance in daily life.

The Spiritual Quest for Meaning

The quest for purpose endures despite life's seemingly limitless options. In this section, we set out on a spiritual journey to discover the deeper meaning behind our very being.

What Is Spiritual Enlightenment Really About?

Explore the fundamentals of spiritual awakening and the importance of establishing a connection with one's inner or higher self.

Discovering Your Spiritual Journey

Discover a route that connects with your search for purpose and fulfillment by investigating a variety of spiritual traditions, philosophies, and belief systems.

The Function of Ethics and Values

Recognize the crucial place that morals and values play in your spiritual development. They act as guiding ideas that show you the way to inner fulfillment.

Practises of Mindfulness and Meditation

A path to great inner serenity and self-discovery is opened up through the practice of meditation and mindfulness. We explore these practices' potential for transformation in this section.

The Technique of Mediation

Learn the art of meditation by developing a regular practice that gives your life clarity and peace, starting with setting aims and choosing the appropriate technique.

Daily Mindfulness Practise

Learn how to incorporate mindfulness into your daily activities so that you can appreciate and feel each moment more fully.

The Meditational Pathway to the Inner World

Discover how meditation can help you connect with your most profound desires, values, and objectives by taking you on an inner journey of self-discovery.

Obtaining Balance and Harmony in Life

Harmony and balance in life are crucial for the pursuit of limitless potential. You are led on the way to balancing the numerous facets of your existence in this part.

Managing Work and Personal Life

Acquire the skill of juggling work obligations with personal well-being and family obligations to promote more equilibrium and happiness.

Building Positive Relationships

Investigate the nuances of developing satisfying and harmonious relationships with friends, family, and loved ones to add more connections to your life.

Taking Care of Your Physical and Mental Health

Put your health and well-being first by implementing habits that improve your quality of life overall, reduce stress, and support good health.

Embracing the Outdoors and Nature

Find consolation in the natural rhythms of life and the restorative power of nature and the outdoors by reconnecting with your surroundings.

Conclusion: Chapter 7 of The Inner Infinite invites you to embark on a spiritual journey that goes beyond the limits of the physical universe. By connecting with your inner self, accepting the transformational power of meditation and mindfulness, and balancing the various elements of your existence, you can embark on a path to discover deeper meaning and fulfillment. Your journey culminates in the inner infinite, where you learn that life's limitless potential extends not only externally but also internally.

Chapter 8: Transitioning to a New Chapter

Transitions are the chapters that determine our evolution in the lifelong journey. In Chapter 8, "Transitioning to a New Chapter," the author offers advice on how to embrace change, find new hobbies and passions, and navigate life transitions with confidence.

Navigating Life Transitions with Confidence

Our path is a tapestry of shifts, and how we move through them determines who we are. We go into the skill of accepting change with confidence in this section.

Knowing About Life Transitions

Discover the numerous life transitions—from job changes and moves to personal milestones—and their enormous effects on personal development.

Developing Flexibility

Learn the importance of adaptation and resilience in the face of transitions and get useful building blocks for these essential abilities.

Making Decisions Effectively in Transitions

Learn to make wise judgments in transitions, making sure that each one is in line with your changing ambitions.

Finding new passions and interests

Transitions allow for the emergence of fresh possibilities and passions. This section explores the process of identifying and fostering new passions.

Curiosity and exploration

Explore unexplored territory and reawaken your sense of wonder as you discover interests you may not have known you had.

Accept the idea of passion projects—creative endeavors that, regardless of your skill level, provide joy and fulfillment to your life.

To weave a tapestry of varied experiences, learn how to establish a harmonious balance between the continuation of your former interests and the acceptance of new hobbies.

Embracing the Possibilities of Change

Change is not just a phase to go through; it is a world of opportunities. This section delves into the practice of fully accepting change's transforming character.

Change as a Growth Catalyst

Recognize change as a powerful force that pulls you towards the infinite and serves as a catalyst for your personal growth and development.

Perspectives on Change Reframed

Learn how changing your attitude towards change may turn it from a cause of uncertainty into a journey with boundless possibility.

Learn the skill of letting go of the past, letting go of attachments that no longer serve you, and allowing new opportunities to enter your life.

Conclusion: Your Path to Endless Possibilities

It's time to consider our life-changing adventure as we come to the end of this limitless odyssey through the chapters of "Unlocking Infinity: Your Path to Endless Possibilities." As we approach the book's final chapter, we have reached a turning point that signals not an end but a new beginning. This book has served as a guiding star, illuminating the road to your boundless potential.

Summary of Important Takeaways

You have explored the core of self-discovery, innovation, and personal growth via these pages, unearthing the untapped resources of your potential. Let's take a moment to review the main points you should remember as you move forward:

1. **Unlocking infinite:** You now understand that the idea of infinite isn't just limited to numbers; it's also a mental condition. We have access to the infinite's tremendous resources all around us.

2. **Growth Thinking:** Changing from a fixed mindset to a growth mindset gives you the

confidence to face challenges, take lessons from failures, and keep moving forward.

3. **Fostering Positivity:** Positivity and an open mind attract opportunity. Positivity is a powerful tool for attracting abundance into your life.

4. **Overcoming Limitations:** You've looked into any restrictions you may have placed on yourself and have learned how to overcome them.

5. **Creativity Unleashed:** You have unlimited creative potential. There are now ways to break through creative barriers and access limitless inspiration.

6. **The Power of Innovation:** You understand how technology and innovation are more than just tools; they are powerful forces that advance your career and personal journeys.

7. **Spiritual Quest:** In the search for purpose, spirituality, mindfulness, and meditation all provide deep connections with your inner self

that point you in the direction of inner fulfillment.

8. **Accepting Change:** Transitions are stepping stones to new chapters rather than roadblocks. You've mastered the capacity to adjust to change with curiosity and a positive outlook.

Promoting Readers' Acceptance of Their Infinite Potential

The trip now goes on. Your compass is comprised of the wisdom you've attained, the perceptions you've gathered, and the inspiration that has been kindled within you. We urge you to apply these lessons to your life, incorporate them into your routine, and recognize the limitless potential you possess. Your journey is a tapestry of potentialities, and each step you take is woven with the threads of change, development, and self-discovery.

Your Path to Endless Possibilities Starts Right Now

Your journey to countless opportunities starts right now, in this very second. It's time for you to embark on your special journey using the information you've gained, the inspiration you've tapped into, and the inner strength you've developed. The pages of your life are ready to be written, and each one offers you a fresh chance to discover the infinite.

You are the author of your story, the artist of your painting, and the navigator of your journey, this is the final message we leave you with as we part ways at the end of this book. Unlock the infinity that dwells within you, accept change, embrace challenges, and take a brave step into the countless opportunities that lie ahead.

Your journey has just started.

Appendix: Supplemental Materials, Exercises, and Suggested Reading

The appendix is a veritable gold mine of tools, activities, and suggested readings to help you on your way to realizing your limitless potential. You can find a plethora of resources here to broaden your knowledge, discover your potential, and carry on your search for limitless opportunities.

Further Resources

You'll find a variety of supplementary materials in this section to help you on your path to self-discovery, innovation, and personal development.

1. Apps for mindfulness and meditation: Look through a list of suggested apps that might help you develop your relaxation, mindfulness, and meditation skills.

2. Online Learning Platforms: Locate a carefully curated list of online learning platforms that provide courses on a variety of topics to aid in the development of your knowledge and skills.

3. Resources for Professional Development: Find websites, forums, and communities that are dedicated to your personal and professional growth so you may interact with others who share your interests and gain access to important knowledge.

4. Inspirational Podcasts: Tune in to podcasts from thought leaders, businesspeople, and artists for inspiration, motivation, and insights.

5. Access a collection of tools and software to improve your capacity for innovative thinking and creative thinking.

Activities and Next Steps

The activities and concrete steps in this section are meant to help you apply the ideas and concepts discussed in the book to your own life.

1. Keep an infinite mindset journal to reflect on your present outlook and to create goals for fostering an infinite mentality in different spheres of your life.

2. Creative Ideation Exercise: Take part in an exercise that will help you come up with new ideas for your professional and personal endeavors.

3. Mindfulness Practise Guide: Develop a daily mindfulness routine by following a step-by-step

mindfulness practice guide to foster inner tranquillity and self-awareness.

4. Goal Setting and Action Planning: Make a structured plan to accomplish your ambitions by using a goal-setting and action-planning template to identify them.

5. Change preparation Assessment: Using a thorough questionnaire, evaluate your preparation for change and apply the results to successfully manage life transitions.

List of suggested readings

With the help of a carefully curated list of suggested texts, broaden your horizons and improve your comprehension. These books provide more information on how to develop yourself, be creative, innovative, spiritual, and deal with change.

1. "Mindset: The New Psychology of Success" by Carol S. Dweck: Learn about the benefits of a growth mindset and the psychology of success.

2. Julia Cameron's "The Artist's Way": Learn about the creative process and discover your artistic potential with the help of this venerable manual.

3. Read "Innovator's Dilemma" by Clayton M. Christensen   learn the disruptive innovation principles and how they affect business and personal development.

4. "The Power of Now" by Eckhart Tolle: This inspirational book will take you on a journey of mindfulness, presence, and spirituality.

5. William Bridges, "Transitions: Making Sense of Life's Changes": Develop a deeper comprehension of life changes and learn how to successfully navigate them.

Keep in mind that your quest to unlock infinity is a continual and dynamic process as you peruse these resources, take on the activities, and delve into the suggested books. Your entryway into a universe of ongoing learning, exploration, and self-transformation is the appendix.